Dreaming Night Terrors

Naomi Ruth Lowinsky

Felton, CA

Dreaming Night Terrors
Copyright ©2020, Naomi Ruth Lowinsky

All rights reserved. Printed in the United States of America. No part of this book may be used or reproduced in any manner whatsoever without written permission except in the case of brief quotations embodied in critical articles and reviews. For information contact:

RIVER SANCTUARY PUBLISHING
P.O Box 1561
Felton, CA 95018
www.riversanctuarypublishing.com

Dedicated to the awakening of the New Earth

BOOK & COVER DESIGN
Melanie Gendron
melaniegendron999@gmail.com

COVER IMAGE
SymphonyFantastique
Intaglio by Bradley Tepaske
www.bradleytepaske.com

AUTHOR PHOTO
Nora Lowinsky

FIRST EDITION

ISBN: 978-1-952194-03-0

To the spirit of my father

Edward Elias Lowinsky

Table of Contents

fragment from "Dream of a City"	1
What I Want to Tell My Mama	2
fragment	5
In the Wild Wake of an American Election	6
fragment	9
Wishing in the Woods With Hillary	10
fragment	13
Me Too	14
fragment	17
On the Mexican Side of the American Wall	18
fragment	21
Ivanka in Hyderabad	22
fragment	25
The Spirit of Elijah Speaks	26
Acknowledgements	29
About the Poet	31

If you are a dream disguised as a city I've dreamt you so often
Dreamt water trance reflecting the black prow slipping through

Dreamt that old dance with a single oar   over the glittering scales
of the always writhing   sea serpent

What I Want To Tell My Mama

Only she's gone   a slight rustle of reeds
at the edge of the pond   a paw print in the mud

Sometimes she takes my hand   like a curious
two year old   tracing my veins   touching my rings

Mutti   you've dived down below   your German
gutterals   found your own   Ur tongue

   Crim crutz
   Olam Bolam

If you were who you used to be   Mama
I'd tell you about that Scary Man

that Chaos Man   with Caterwauling Hair   who beats
his chest and threatens

to drive us back
into the Tohu Bohu

He'd build a Golden Wall   high as the Great Wall
of China   Impenetrable as Negative Space

A Magnificent Wall to keep the likes of us
Refugees and our Rabble children   out

of America   Mama   he's a Huckster
a Big Hunk of Catastrophe

Flasher Man   Slash Her Man
Hair sprayed into Caesar's Brass Helmet

  Olam Bolam
  Crimini Crutz

All the ghosts we keep in the closet
rush in shrieking

  "It's the Nazis
  It's the Fascists
  It's the Cossacks
  It's the Huns
  It's Joseph McCarthy as Hair Spray Man
  come to eat our young   Run!"

He is the King of the Hoax   the Prince of Evasion
Makes sausage

of our worst fears
We eat it

What he eats
is cotton candy

  Rim Ram
  Crimini hachts

There's a gargantuan Wall of Broken
Glass   between his lovers   and his haters

yet we are spell bound   Mama
How can I explain

He has hula dancer fingers
He curls them

unfurls them
We watch   mesmerized

"On Day One   Hour One
You'll all be gone   Every last one of you
                            Enemy Aliens!"

   Crimini crumini
   Olam Bolam

Mama   make him
be gone…

Some say you're a fabrication   a city of stones stolen
from other people's cities

a flood pretending you are paradise
tied to a forest of long beams that pierce   the sea bottom

In the Wild Wake of an American Election

I. Dark Matter

The question wakes you in the night
What if your worst fears are the story of our time?

In the surgery waiting room   worst fears bloom   The TV is
on mute   The smart phone is a portal   an oracle   a hideout

The Word of the Year 2016   says Face Book   *is "surreal"*
Trust natural law say the cards   *Surrender   to the black hole*

They're closing all the shops   It's crazy out there
Last night in a dream   Obama sat on the edge   of a black hole

Twitter man is on TV   big and imposing   riding down his golden
                                                    escalator   His hair
gleams gold   his tower gleams gold   his tie gleams red   hangs low
                                           a great schlong of a tie

What do they mean "Not our President"?   *He won*   *That's how it
                                                                works*
Dark matter can't be seen   touched   smelled   heard   tasted   Is it in us?

II. Dark Energy

Some wait to be called   into the dark   Some wait   for their
                                                        someone
to emerge   from twilight sleep   the knife   the black hole

She fingers her sapphire blue headscarf   sees her grandmother
                                            smile   long ago
in Aleppo   Prays she will see her again   *Inshallah*   in this life
Her husband can't face the jinni   in her body   the jinni that's
                                                                eating
America   Same jinni devoured   the Arab Spring

Some of us have ghosts in our head   shrieking worst case
                                                          scenarios
Dark energy makes up most of the universe   We don't know what it is

She's huddled in the ruby red sweater   he gave her   Tells
                                                             herself
Don't go there   Don't think about where   they will cut him
The worst has already happened   to your ancestors   to Emmet Till
                                                           Trayvon Martin
Michael Brown   to nine good souls in Charleston   What did the Bible
                                                                tell them?

Just watch the silent TV   cling to your phone   wait for the door
                                                to open   the nurse
to call your name   take you to your sweet   groggy   someone

He holds her purse   her diamond wedding band   follows the
                                               trail of the Alt Right
on line   Wonders   is there is a cosmic connection   between his
                                                wife's endangered breast
and the turn the country has taken?   How does he get through
                                                the hours   with her
in the dark?   *Mr Road Map to Hitler   keep your hands off my wife*

The baby in the stroller holds his mother's iphone   His eyes
                                            open wide   What is he seeing?
Success through what is small   So says The Book of Changes

III. Dark Time

The Kali Yuga say the Hindus *is a dark age lacks holy law*
a time of hubris greed war

The President of Tweets tweets *Time to expand our nuclear capacity*
Now there's a worst fear

Doesn't he know our nukes are on hair trigger alert?
He thinks he's in a movie This is real life

Chaos has awoken from a long nap
is putting on dancing shoes and heading for the streets

Unmute the tube   The women warriors are on   Rachel in a
                                                              black jacket is pushy
A lot of people are hiding under the bed right now   Are we really going
                                                              back to the arms race?
KellyAnne   in black velvet with cleavage   smiles sweetly
Nothing like that   He just wants us all to be safe

The fruits of peace outweigh the plunder of war   So says Obama still
                                                              our president
Let there be an arms race tweets the President of Tweets   as
                                                              though to say

Let the wild rumpus begin

When black holes collide there are no handrails   Let go say the Runes
of the world as you know it of the world as you want it to be   Old
                                                              skins must be shed

If you're an enchantment   masquerading as a holiday
complete with fish market and sparkling wine

I could be   remembering
my life as a woman   in somebody else's dream

Wishing in the Woods   With Hillary

I wish you'd surprise me   in the woods   Hillary   as you did
that young mother   baby daughter on her back
                                           the day after we lost you
for president   She took a selfie   My daughter sent me the link
Who will we be without you   in your moon bright pantsuit?
Who will stand up to the strongman   when Michelle and Barack
walk out of the White House   and speak to us only in dreams?

My wish is to see you among trees   their leaves gone gold
and crimson   or dry and dead on the earth   Your little dog
will sniff me   And you   who've been pilloried
your goodness debunked   as though working
for women and children   lacks gravitas   As though gravitas
is a loaded scrotum   whose natural enemy   is a woman with
                                                         powers

Mother trudged from father's study   to kitchen   to bathroom
and back when he whistled   I kid you not   He whistled   She typed
his manuscripts   cooked   bathed children   darned socks   Hillary
She was the air we breathed   the water we swam in
the earth we walked on   our hearth   our heart beat
Her powers invisible   to the kingdom of men   But O

she was fierce   about voting for you in '08
Now she's lost   her way in the woods
lost my name   your fame   lost the whole world
of visible powers   lost to the outcry
the pandemonium   the kids walking out
of their schools shouting   "Not Our President"

The trees raise their boughs   and prophesy
When the moon comes closer to earth
than it's been since the year you were born
the haters will crawl out from under their rocks
the "white only" nation come out of the woodwork
You won't know whose country you're in

Maybe our time is over   Hillary   All that e-mail evil
because you're attached to your old familiar   that Blackberry
you refuse to waste time   learning new smartphones   I'm with
                                                                                        you
But my dear   the world is passing us by   That young mother
in the woods   after we lost you for president   posted you
and her baby daughter on Facebook   It went viral   My
daughter sent me the link

Hillary   my wish is to surround you   with sisters
of the secret grove   We'll sit in a circle   kiss the earth
with our holiest lips   We'll lift up our hands and pray
for your healing   our healing   the healing of the dis–
respected   disaffected   molested   undocumented   Jim Crowed
And let's not forget   the trees   the bees   the buffalo

We'll breathe into our bellies   Our backbones grow
into strong tree trunks   our roots descend   While I'm wishing
let's throw in a chorus of frogs   and the smell
of the earth after rain   For it's downgoing time   in America
underworld time   time to hide out in a cave
How I wish for your company in the dark   Hillary

We'll make a fire   talk story   remember our mothers'
invisible powers   Maybe we'll sink into dreamtime   Maybe
                                                Michelle
will visit She'll wear a wonderful dress remind us of grace of joy
She'll speak from her heart   *Though the weather's becoming*
a banshee goddess   Though the "white only" nation
is trolling the web   Though the emperor elect

is tweeting our downfall   My wish is   Remember
The way of women   is our way   The moon swells
the moon goes dark   pulling the tides   in and out
The way of the trees   is our way   So raise up
your branches   sisters   for we are one   gathering
Soon sap   will rise   apple trees flower

We'll weave us a canopy   all over this land
It will be uprising time   once again
 in America

the always writhing serpent   below
you floating you moonchild you changeling playing   the tides

young couples   dressed for the glittering
gliding under old bridges   through   the full circle

Me Too
        September 27th 2018

All of us are you   Christine   in this moment
All of us in tears   because that's what we do when we're mad
All of us took off the day   to watch you tell
what few of us have ever dared to tell
All of our eyes dart   from senator   to prosecutor
Prosecutor?   Whose nightmare is this?

Some of us watched Anita Hill   face those same   white men
those same   dead fish eyes   a generation ago   Anita was so
self possessed   Not one hair   went astray   in her careful do
while your scared hair   Christine   blows around   tangles
in your eye glass frames   tries to hide
the terrified fifteen year old in you we all are
For who of us has not felt   that heavy hand   over our mouth
Who of us has not feared   death by suffocation?
Who of us has not heard   that nasty laughter?

Shirley Chisholm locked herself in chambers   Wept her rage
at those old boys   who dismissed   diminished   betrayed her
They could not tolerate   a black woman   running for president
Who of us did not feel   primordial fear   when Hillary spoke up
while the guy with that schlong of a tie   stalked her   mocked her
Who of us did not feel   the hot tongs   of the Inquisitor
when in the Quicken Loans Arena   in Cleveland   in 2016
a guy with a tie incited the crowd to   "Lock Her Up!"   "Lock
                                                                             Her Up!"

All of us know what happens   to those who refuse to do
the patriarchal dance   of diffidence
We're stalked   pilloried   diagnosed as disturbed
in the womb   We bleed from our eyes

Well you're showing them   Christine   not one iota
of rage   not a drop   of disturbance   You make sweet and pliant
eye contact   name your terror   though sometimes we glimpse
the owl in your soul   how your roots reach down   to your own
                                                                                    hard truth

You're a flower in a fierce wind   pulling petals in close   until
storm over   goddess willing   you rise
to your full stature   dismiss the security detail   return
to your everyday home   with its two front doors   teach
psychology   make dinner   walk the dog   help the boys
with their homework

But this is not the end of it   Your dance of diffidence
settles nothing He's back   the one we all remember from forever
beating his chest   roaring   No one stops
his predatory attack   his entitled engorgement   for which we are
a handy piece of flesh   to be grabbed   groped   banged   nailed
to a broken
                                          branch
                                                    of the tree

All of us know   what he's not saying
that we're witches   bitches   we are   let's say it aloud
CUNTS   And what is a cunt   but a portal   into a new world
we all come through   unless Caesar gets his way
and what is a witch   but a woman of power
who knows her own nature   is a part of all nature

In my dream   a brilliant black girl paints the world   in every living color
She's Changing Woman   Woman of the Craft   Woman becoming us all
She runs strong   as a wild horse   dodges rocks and fissures   Maybe
it's your dream Christine   and we're all with you   on the wings of the owl
in the deepest part of the woods   where the oak grove remembers
the ones we were before
                         we were grabbed   groped   banged   nailed

Dreamt lion devoured me for love   of narrow passages
ended by stone walls   sudden canals   someone's footsteps
                                                behind me

Dreamt water's lilting loveliness becoming land becoming water
Dreamt night terrors in the lion's mouth

On the Mexican Side of the American Wall

The mountains   old familiars   misty blue drifters   jungle enfolded
they comfort us and then   there's the sea   umbilical beat
of the great mother's heart

We've been coming here for twelve years   or is it thirteen?
We've grown old   visiting this village   Only this time is different
America's dream has been busted

The auction block   the shackles   show through
The Mexican president refuses to meet with our incoming tyrant
Why should *he* pay   for America's

twenty billion dollar wall?   We need sanctuary
At breakfast   the Canadians wonder
"Why don't you just stay down here?"   We sat in this same

Great Hall   during the Bush years   watching the moods
of the ocean and sky   the frigates soar   the pelicans swoop
and raged   about government by the rich

for the rich   Shock and Awe   The treasures of Sumer
looted and lost   a culture destroyed
and all those young Americans   who came home   shattered

This time is different   Bush would never have banned Muslims
Anguish and rage   at the airports   on Facebook   on Twitter
in e-mails from everyone we know

Someone says   "Government by fiat"   We wonder   Is it a coup?
Is it a smoke screen?   Does he want power
for a billion years   like the former president of Gambia?

Disconnect   Listen to the surf   watch the palm trees wave their fronds
The talk is of sharks   The time he was swimming
with his daughter   and someone shouted "Great White!"

On the beach the waves are huge
surfers' delight   If we knew how to ride waves
would that help?

The ocean opens her great goddess mouth
She raises her ancient head
beats her fists on the sand

She's taking it back   our beach   for sand castles
for baring our breasts to the sun   for releasing baby turtles
protected by human children   as they run   to the sea

Meanwhile in Berkeley   the students protest the Alt–right
When did that word arrive?   Anarchists dressed like Ninjas
invade Sproul Plaza   break glass   start fires   *Mario Savio*
                                              Where are you?

The bigot in chief would defund the University   First the Muslims
then the academics   *If mother   hadn't lost her grip   on what's new
who's in charge   She'd feel like a Jewish child in Deutschland   all over again*

We wander the beach   looking for ocean
smoothed rocks   to fit   in the palm of a hand
to sooth a troubled soul   calm an angry heart

At the lagoon   a congregation of turkey vultures
The ducks flutter their wings   close to hummingbird speed
They levitate   A dog leaps in and out of the water   ecstatic

This is the lagoon the local rich guy tried to hijack
fill it in   build a resort   The people said "No!"   You can't
interfere with a waterway"   Standing Rock   in San Pancho

Bad night   Sleep slinks away   Mosquito bites itch
House moans   *An Arab boy   or is he Mexican*
howls his fury   hurls his stones   at the big   bad   American wall

At the bar   David shows Julio how to make a Mezcal Martini
Breaking down walls   with spirits   There is dancing in the streets
of San Pancho   to American Rock and Roll

The leader of the band   dedicates the next song to   "El Loco
en la Casa Blanca"   "Stop children   what's that sound?
Everybody look   what's going down"

Come the Muslim registry we'll be Muslims
What if we can't travel?
What if we can never come here again?   Where the sickle moon
and Venus   commune in the velvet night

Where our days   fall into easy patterns   and we return
to our old wild selves   Where every evening
we watch the sunset   You would not believe the glory

we've seen   Imagine this   rays of sun through clouds
like a blessing   Sun disappears in a streak of gray   is born again
dies again   is born yet again   a glowing globe   and then
                                        the green flash

Some say you're a swamp   dressed up as a fancy lady
all feather boas and gilded mirrors

I think you are a masked ball   dancing to songs
our parents sang   before they'd even dreamt us

Ivanka in Hyderabad

Glamour queen of your father's brand   you tower
over Prime Minister Modi hold forth about promoting prosperity
for women entrepreneurs   in the former palace of the Nizam
now a five–star hotel   in the City of Pearls
not far from where I lived lifetimes ago   You reign
in midnight blue   you dazzle
with sequins   and metallic flowers   That gown
costs three thousand five hundred dollars   would take three years
working in one of your clothing line sweatshops to earn
So says the screen   of my MacBook Air
where it is written   the town folk are fuming and twittering

Just now only   Ivanka Trump Road   is all fixed up
beggars and stray dogs   disappeared   rainbows painted
on tree trunks   to greet the motorcade   just now only
our road's the same as always   potholes and garbage   Ivanka
please come to our house   We bow to the goddess within you

That would be Lakshmi   Lotus lady   Queen of abundance
Lady of jewels and of pollen   Mother of the World
She doesn't dwell in temples   but in the homes of the lucky
She taught me how to wrap a sari   when I was twenty something
how to walk up stairs   in the long flow of silk   without tripping
She churned the oceans of my first world mind   with glass
                                                        bangles
ankle bells   flower offerings   threshold magic
Colors that clash in America   make wild love
on the dark skin of women   who carry rocks   build roads
shape cow dung   into patties   to fuel their kitchen fires

Back then   Hyderabad was a sleepy Muslim town
swarming with Hindu deities   where sacred cows dozed
in the dusty roads   bicycle rickshaws rang their bells
vegetable wallahs sang their wares   the occasional car   honked
Now   it's a tech hub   They call it Cyberabad
Ivanka   have you ever met   Lakshmi's dreaded Elder Sister
Lady of bad luck   torment   trouble   poverty?
I hadn't   before I lived here   hadn't touched   the scaly skin
of a child with kwashiorkor   her hair gone rusty
her stick–thin arms and legs   her swollen belly
until I met Rani   whose name means queen   baby daughter
of scrawny Sheela   who swept my floors   squatted in the
                                                    kitchen
removing the rocks from the rice   I made it my business
to feed them well   What happened
after I was gone?   Did Rani survive?
Sheela had five   lost three   wept with me
for Rose Kennedy   when Bobbie   was assassinated
Rani   would be older than you   Ivanka   by a generation
Maybe she has a daughter   who works in a sweatshop
for one of your women entrepreneurs   just now only
she's been harassed   assaulted   called a donkey   a dog
can't feed her children on slave wages   Lakshmi doesn't come
to her house   Every year   at Deepavali   she lights lamps
beats pots and pans   to drive   the Elder Sister away
She makes intricate designs   at the threshold
to invite the jeweled goddess in   Ivanka   I hear you've tried
to influence your fire and fury father   he who throws
lightning bolts for sport   You've spoken up for the earth
for women who've been   assaulted   raped   demeaned

Lakshmi says
When no sacrifice is made   the sun and the moon
lose their glow   the gods lose   their magic

Meanwhile   your brawling   rapacious father   is ripping up
the fabric of America   wildlife refuge   tribal treaties   dreamers
the safety net   the Bill of Rights   a woman's power   over her own
magic threshold   Meanwhile the Elder Sister   is given a seat
at the table   She reigns   despite all our first world wealth
over hungry children   slave wages   cold weather evictions
opioid addiction   detention   deportation   and the rich grow
                                                                    richer

Ivanka   you too are a mother   you too have a daughter
Come with me   just now only   to visit a home in Hyderabad
on a road where beggars sleep   mangy dogs roam   We pass over
intricate floral designs   created by women   at the threshold
of a small room   lit by candles   in clay jars   We bring garlands
of marigolds   sweets for the children   We bow to the goddess
in Rani   in her daughter   her granddaughters
We burn incense   add our voices to their puja

O Mother of the World   Lady of Abundance   Queen of Delight
and of Harmony   You who sit on a lotus flower   in an ocean of milk
whose breasts glow   whose conch shell holds the mysteries
of pollen   of tides   You who kindle kindness   truth telling
The Golden Rule   Enter our hearts   reveal to us
                                What sacrifice   is required?

There is a garden   a fruit tree   a snake
                         with the head of a woman

a black prow slipping through
our water trance   over the always writhing
sea serpent

The Spirit of Elijah Speaks

October 17th, 2019
Our children are the living messengers we send into a future we will never see.

—Elijah Cummings

Open the door   I'm here to haunt   the House
I didn't mean to leave you all   in the lurch
Covenants broken   The Constitution   under siege
My time has expired   I beg you   guard this moment

I didn't mean to leave you all   in the lurch
Been signing subpoenas   to the end   of my breath
My time has expired   I beg you   guard this moment
What will you do   to protect   our democracy?

Been signing subpoenas   to the end   of my breath
Was called to earth   to speak truth   to abuse
What will you do   to protect   our democracy?
I come from sharecroppers   Our ancestors   were slaves

Was called to earth   to speak truth   to abuse
Became Master of the House   and Chair   of Oversight
I come from sharecroppers   Our ancestors   were slaves
Was shown the glory   of the separation   of powers

Became Master of the House   and Chair   of Oversight
Thou shalt not separate children   from parents   seeking asylum
Behold the glory   of the separation   of powers
Thou shalt not arouse the crowd's   bad blood   high dudgeon

Thou shalt not separate children in cages   leave them sitting in
                                                                         feces
We're better than that
Thou shalt not arouse the crowd's   bad blood   high dudgeon
Who will speak truth   to the Master   of Mendacity?

We're better than that
He has slandered   the people   of my home city   Baltimore
Who will speak truth   to the Master   of Mendacity?
You've got only   one life   and within you   a small   still   voice

He has slandered   the people   of my home city   Baltimore
The Forefathers warned us   Beware of demagogues
Does he ever listen   to that small   still   voice?
Look in the mirror poet   that haunt in your eyes   is the spirit
                                                                        of your father

This demagogue   this walking catastrophe   has roused me   from the dead
Look in the mirror America   that haunt in your eyes   is me   your
                                                                        ancestral refugee
Never break your covenant   with Lady Liberty   Guard The Constitution
My name is Elijah   Open the door

Acknowledgements

With many thanks to the editors of the following publications in which some of these poems have appeared:

After The Pause: In the Wild Wake of An American Election, On the Mexican Side of the American Wall, Wishing in the Woods with Hillary

PoetryMagazine.com: Dream of a City

Psychological Perspectives: Me Too, The Spirit of Elijah Speaks

Deep gratitude to Susan Terris, who inspired this chapbook and helped prepare it.

Much gratitude to Brad TePaske whose Intaglio *Symphonie Fantastique* is the cover image.

I am forever grateful to Melanie Grendon, who designed the cover and handled the logistics of publication.

About the Poet

Naomi Ruth Lowinsky comes from a family of refugees who fled Nazi Germany. Her poetry has always engaged the political, but during the Trump era it has become an emotional necessity to make poems out of night terrors. A widely published and anthologized poet she is the winner of the Blue Light Poetry Prize as well as the Obama Millennial Prize. Her fourth poetry collection *The Faust Woman Poems* follows one woman's Faustian adventures during the 1960s and '70s, through Women's Liberation and the return of the Goddess.

Lowinsky is a Jungian Analyst and a member of the San Francisco Jung Institute where she has taught a poetry workshop, *Deep River,* for over a decade. Her new book of essays, *The Rabbi, the Goddess and Jung*, contemplates what the Kabbalah calls the "beyond that lies within"—the still small voice of the Self, and the wisdom that comes from dreams and active imagination. She is the Poetry Editor of *Psychological Perspectives*, and blogs about poetry and life at sisterfrombelow.com.

www.ingramcontent.com/pod-product-compliance
Lightning Source LLC
Chambersburg PA
CBHW051720040426
42446CB00008B/980